NATIONAL GEOGRAPHIC KiDS

weird but true! 5

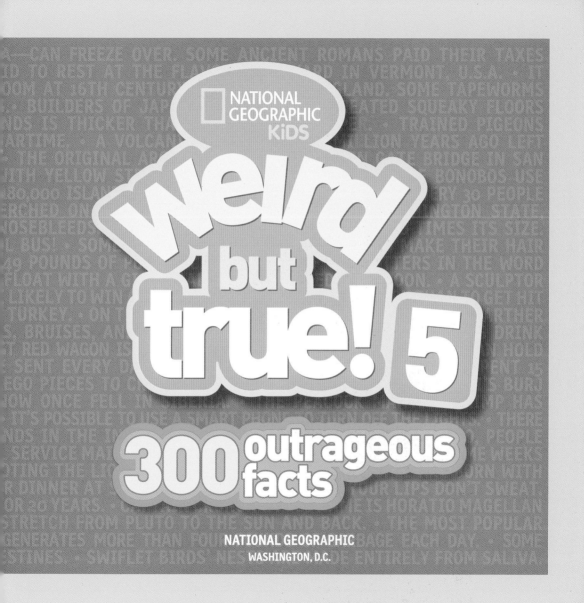

NATIONAL GEOGRAPHIC
KiDS

weird but true! 5

300 outrageous facts

NATIONAL GEOGRAPHIC
WASHINGTON, D.C.

Visit us online:
Kids: kids.nationalgeographic.com
Parents: nationalgeographic.com/books
Teachers: ngchildrensbooks.org
Librarians: ngchildrensbooks.org

Library of Congress Control
    Number: 2012956100

ISBN (Trade): 978-1-4263-1124-6
ISBN (Library): 978-1-4263-1125-3
ISBN (Scholastic): 978-1-4263-1633-3

Printed in the United States of America
13/QGT-CML/2

The world's biggest **skateboard** is almost as long as **a school bus!**

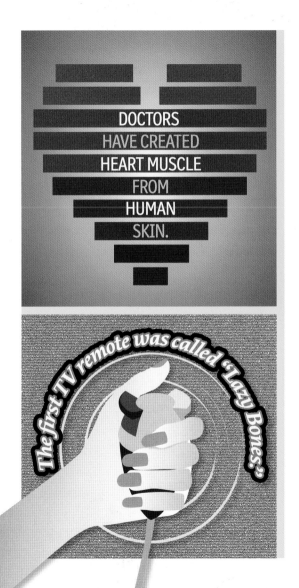

DOCTORS HAVE CREATED HEART MUSCLE FROM HUMAN SKIN.

The first TV remote was called 'Lazy Bones.'

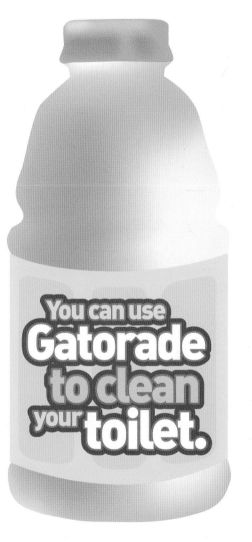

You can use Gatorade to clean your toilet.

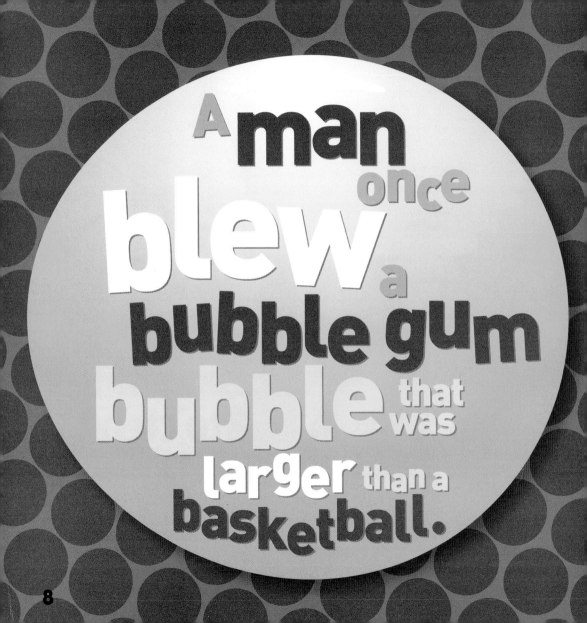

A man once blew a bubble gum bubble that was larger than a basketball.

There's more **salt** in one gallon of (3.79 L) **sea water** than in **49 pounds** (22.3 kg) of **potato chips!**

A GROUP OF HIPPOS IS SOMETIMES CALLED A BLOAT.

A **VENDING MACHINE** IN SINGAPORE **GAVE AWAY A FREE SODA** TO ANYONE WHO **HUGGED THE MACHINE.**

Giraffe hooves are the size of dinner plates.

ALL OF THE LETTERS IN THE WORD "TYPEWRITER"

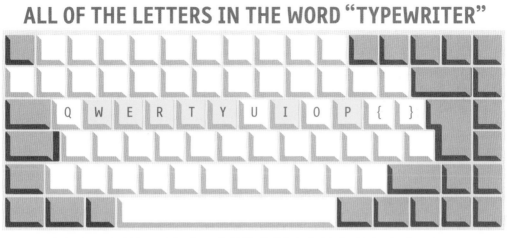

Q W E R T Y U I O P { }

CAN BE FOUND IN ONE ROW ON A KEYBOARD.

HOT WATER CAN FREEZE FASTER THAN COLD WATER.

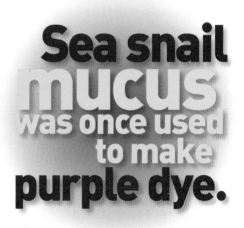

Sea snail mucus was once used to make purple dye.

The first cars didn't have windshield wipers.

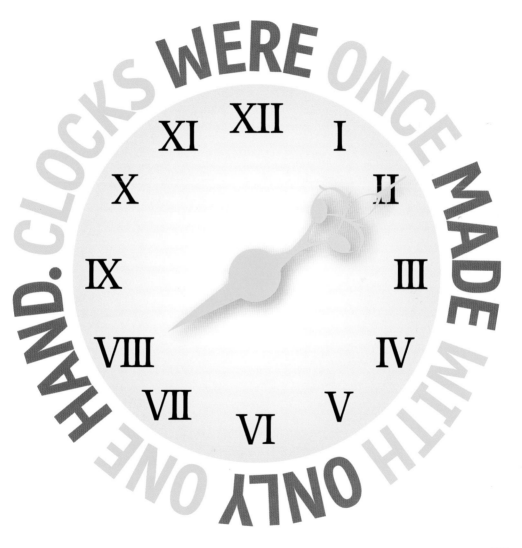

CLOCKS WERE ONCE MADE WITH ONLY ONE HAND.

SHARKS
CAN'T BLINK.

A GERMAN FASHION DESIGNER MAKES CLOTHING FROM MILK POWDER.

GOATS SNACK ON POISON IVY.

There's a **horse** that's so small she sleeps in a **doghouse.**

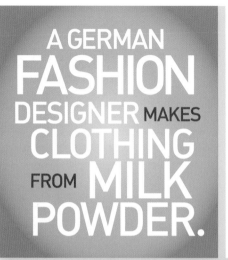

Ostriches can **swim** but they can't fly.

A U.S. ice-cream shop sold insect-flavored ice cream.

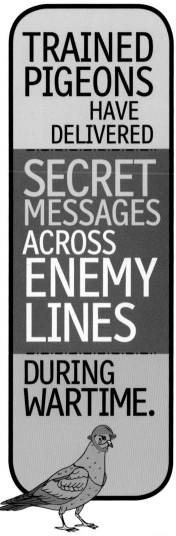

TRAINED PIGEONS HAVE DELIVERED SECRET MESSAGES ACROSS ENEMY LINES DURING WARTIME.

Sticking **raw bacon** in your **nostrils** can stop serious **nosebleeds.**

MALE TURKEYS ARE CALLED **GOBBLERS.**

BEES HAVE FIVE EYES.

SOME BLUEBERRIES ARE **PINK.**

THERE ARE
180,000 ISLANDS

IN FINLAND—

THAT'S ONE FOR ABOUT
EVERY 30 PEOPLE
IN THE COUNTRY.

IN TAIWAN, GARBAGE TRUCKS **BLAST MUSIC** TO REMIND PEOPLE TO BRING OUT THE TRASH.

Some crabs are bright purple.

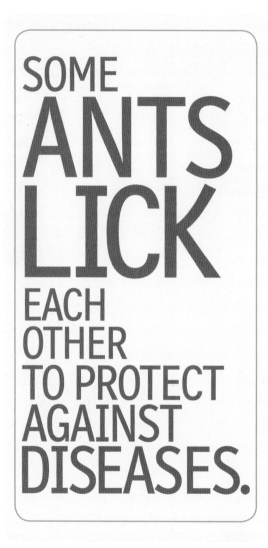

SOME **ANTS LICK** EACH OTHER TO PROTECT AGAINST DISEASES.

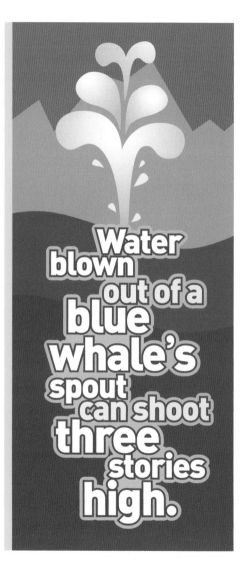

Water blown out of a blue whale's spout can shoot three stories high.

SOME **POLICE OFFICERS** IN CAIRO, EGYPT, PATROL THE **PYRAMIDS** ON **CAMELBACK.**

25

Spider silk is used to make fishing nets in some countries.

Raindrops are shaped like hamburger buns.

A Taiwanese airline **flies Hello Kitty-themed jets.**

Triceratops had up to **800 teeth.**

WHEN IT GETS COLD ENOUGH, **NIAGARA FALLS—** ONE OF THE **LARGEST WATERFALLS** IN NORTH AMERICA— **CAN FREEZE OVER.**

Some wildflowers smell like chocolate.

A CANADIAN WOMAN
RODE A MOTORIZED TOILET
UP TO 46 MILES AN HOUR!
(74 kph)

R.I.P.

RETIRED BEN AND JERRY'S ICE-CREAM FLAVORS ARE LAID TO REST AT THE FLAVOR GRAVEYARD IN VERMONT, U.S.A.

Insect blood can be clear, yellow, or green.

IT CAN BE MORE **SATISFYING** TO SCRATCH AN **ITCH** ON YOUR BACK THAN ON YOUR ARM.

A 35-FOOT-TALL, (10.7 m) INFLATED **ANGRY BIRD** PERCHED ON THE SIDE OF THE SEATTLE SPACE NEEDLE, IN WASHINGTON STATE, U.S.A.

Kinkajous can twist their hind feet **backward** to climb trees.

YOU WOULD WEIGH **ZERO POUNDS** AT THE CENTER OF THE (0 kg) EARTH.

A Welshman's **dog** served as **best man** at his wedding.

IF YOUR TONGUE WAS AS LONG AS A FROG'S, IT WOULD REACH DOWN TO YOUR BELLY BUTTON!

VAMPIRE BATS ARE THE ONLY MAMMALS TO HAVE A BLOOD-ONLY DIET.

A candy company makes **gummy bears** the size of footballs.

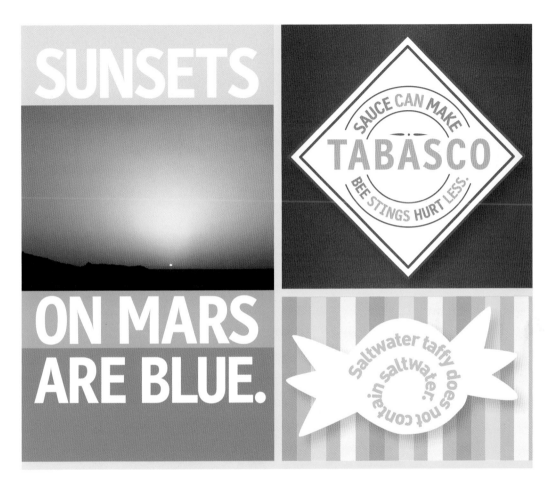

SUNSETS ON MARS ARE BLUE.

TABASCO SAUCE CAN MAKE BEE STINGS HURT LESS.

Saltwater taffy does not contain saltwater.

THERE'S A MILLIPEDE THAT HAS 750 LEGS.

39

FULL MOONS APPEAR BRIGHTER IN WINTER THAN IN SUMMER.

MORE PEOPLE HAVE BEEN TO **THE MOON** THAN TO THE BOTTOM OF THE OCEAN.

SOME BONOBOS USE TOUCH-SCREEN COMPUTERS TO COMMUNICATE WITH HUMANS.

Turtles the size of small cars roamed Earth 60 million years ago.

A leech can suck up five times its body weight in blood.

Thermal vents—cracks in the ocean floor—spew water that's hotter than 750°F. (400°C)

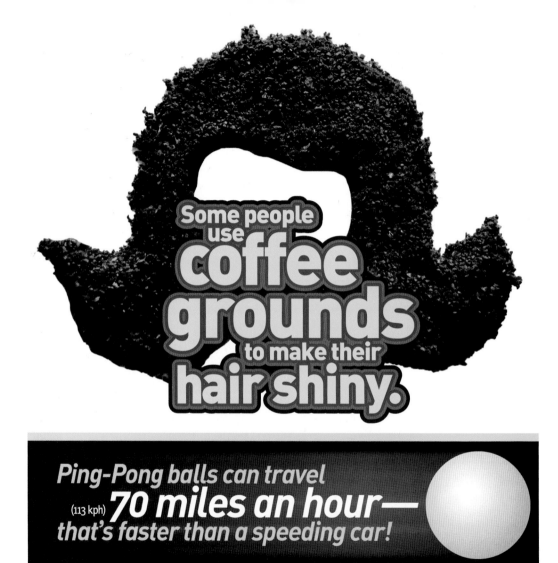

Some people use **coffee grounds** to make their **hair shiny.**

Ping-Pong balls can travel (113 kph) **70 miles an hour—** that's faster than a speeding car!

A building
in South
Korea
is being
built in the
shape of
a pound
sign. #

THE STRONGEST **TORNADOES** ARE PACKED WITH ENOUGH ENERGY TO POWER **10,000 HOUSES** FOR ONE DAY.

A WHITE ORCA WAS SPOTTED IN THE PACIFIC OCEAN.

SOME TARANTULAS ARE BLUE.

You can
buy a wig
for your dog.

BUILDERS OF JAPAN'S NIJO CASTLE CREATED SQUEAKY FLOORS TO PREVENT INTRUDERS FROM SNEAKING IN.

A sea star can turn its stomach inside out.

A baseball stadium in Texas, U.S.A., sold hot dogs that were each longer than two iPads.

ALLIGATOR TEETH

ARE HOLLOW.

53

THE WORLD'S LARGEST BAT HAS A WINGSPAN AS WIDE AS A SOFA.

FINGERPRINTS CAN LAST FOR UP TO 40 YEARS ON PAPER.

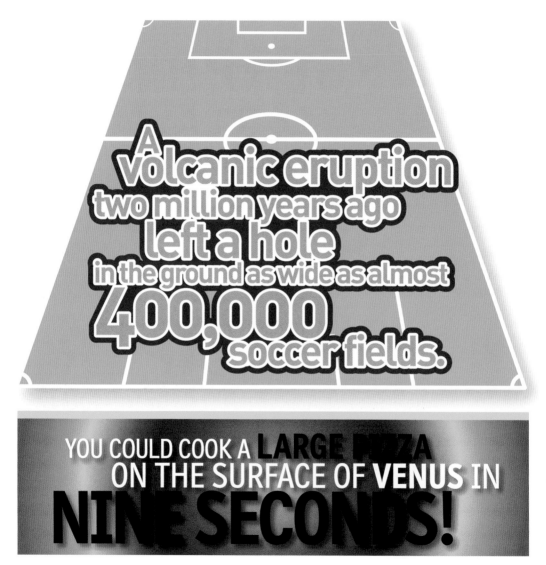

A **volcanic eruption** two million years ago **left a hole** in the ground as wide as almost **400,000** soccer fields.

YOU COULD COOK A **LARGE PIZZA** ON THE SURFACE OF **VENUS** IN **NINE SECONDS!**

Ladybugs might play dead when threatened.

A company in England created cheese-scented perfume.

Babies have taste buds in their cheeks.

Spaceship Earth
at Walt Disney
World Resort in
Florida, U.S.A.,
weighs as much as
17 jumbo
jets.

Whales
have
belly buttons.

A prize **cow** in Canada sold for 1.2 million dollars.

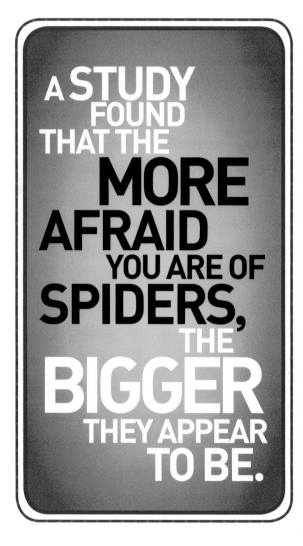

A STUDY FOUND THAT THE **MORE AFRAID** YOU ARE OF **SPIDERS,** THE **BIGGER** THEY APPEAR TO BE.

IN ANCIENT EGYPT ONLY ROYALTY WERE ALLOWED TO EAT MUSHROOMS.

Some **people** are born with a double row of **eyelashes.**

12,345,678,

111,111,111
x111,111,111

987,654,321

Some ancient Romans paid their taxes in honey.

It was considered **good luck** to throw shoes at the bride and groom at 16th-century weddings **in England.**

A **hot drink** can sometimes **cool you down** faster than a **cold drink.**

BEAVERS HAVE A SET OF CLEAR EYELIDS TO SEE UNDERWATER.

UP UNTIL 100 YEARS AGO, SOME **TOOTHBRUSH BRISTLES** WERE MADE FROM **PIG HAIRS.**

SEAWEED CAN **PREVENT** TOOTH DECAY.

Fish sometimes cough.

OOLOGY IS THE STUDY OF BIRD EGGS.

A **pineapple** is actually made up of a **bunch of berries.**

There's a **jellyfish** that can change from an adult back into a baby.

YOUR **BRAIN** CAN HOLD **100 TIMES** MORE INFORMATION THAN A **COMPUTER.**

THE ORIGINAL ARCHITECTS OF THE
GOLDEN GATE BRIDGE
IN SAN FRANCISCO, CALIFORNIA, U.S.A.,
CONSIDERED PAINTING THE BRIDGE
BLACK WITH
YELLOW STRIPES
INSTEAD OF
ORANGE.

A MAN IN
HAVANA, CUBA,
BUILT A BICYCLE
THAT'S AS TALL AS AN ELEPHANT!

Cockroaches recognize members of their family.

400 million tweets are sent every day.

There's a town in Oregon named Boring.

A PARADE FLOAT WITH A GIANT BALLOON IS CALLED A FALLOON.

ACTUAL BUILDING IN DUBAI, UAE.

IT TOOK **450,300 LEGO BRICKS** TO CREATE AN 18-FOOT-TALL (5.5 m) REPLICA OF THE WORLD'S TALLEST BUILDING!

ASTRA

IS THE FEAR OF

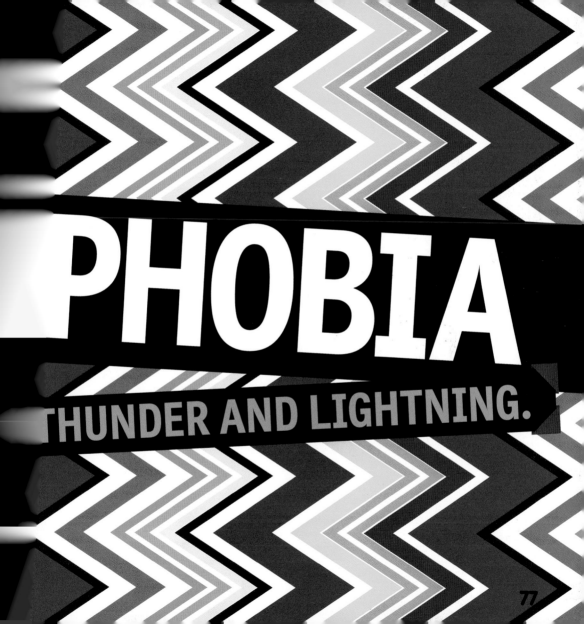

PHOBIA

THUNDER AND LIGHTNING.

A chameleon's **tongue** can travel as fast as **13 miles** (21 kph) **an hour.**

An insect called an **assassin bug** sometimes carries **dead ants on its back to appear bigger.**

Three back-to-back **strikes** in bowling is called a **turkey.**

Elephants drink the equivalent of **800 glasses of water** a day.

Only female mosquitoes bite.

Whale blubber was once used to make margarine.

THE WORLD'S LARGEST RED WAGON IS TALLER THAN A
TWO-STORY BUILDING
AND CAN HOLD 75 KIDS.

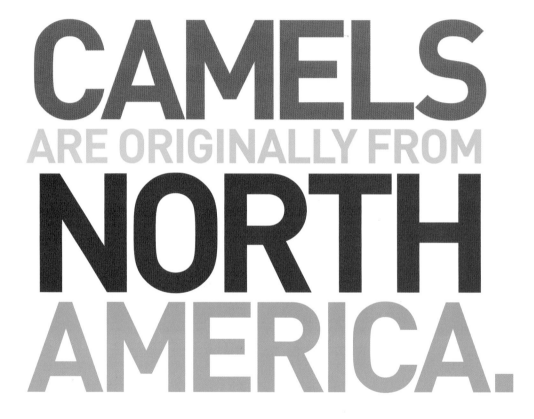

CAMELS ARE ORIGINALLY FROM NORTH AMERICA.

AMERICANS ARE MORE LIKELY TO **WIN A MILLION DOLLARS IN THE LOTTERY** THAN TO GET HIT BY **LIGHTNING.**

9 23 9 8 18 11

ON THE MOON YOU CAN THROW A BALL **SIX** TIMES FARTHER THAN YOU CAN ON EARTH.

BABY EELS ARE CALLED ELVERS.

An **octopus** can detach **an arm** on purpose and then **regrow** it.

The symbol **&**, which means **"and,"** was once a letter in the **English alphabet.**

You can buy **an energy bar with crickets** inside.

YOU CAN SEE A GLASS FROG'S HEART BEATING THROUGH ITS SKIN.

You will likely get **10,000** small cuts, bruises, and sprains in your lifetime.

A BUZZ LIGHTYEAR ACTION FIGURE SPENT 15 MONTHS ON THE INTERNATIONAL SPACE STATION.

89

An elephant's **heart** can weigh as much as a basset hound.

A LION'S **ROAR** IS LOUDER THAN A **LAWN MOWER.**

AGGRESSOR

YOU CAN TELL THE **PERSONALITY** OF SOME **FINCHES** BY THE **COLOR OF THEIR HEADS**— BIRDS WITH BLACK HEADS ARE RISK-TAKERS WHILE REDHEADS ARE MORE AGGRESSIVE.

RISK-TAKER

In Japan you can buy octopus-flavored ice cream.

Orange snow once fell in Siberia.

Some millipedes glow in the dark.

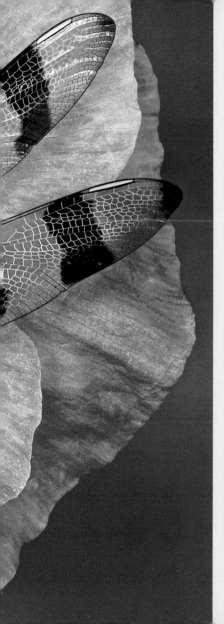

300 MILLION YEARS AGO, **DRAGONFLIES HAD WINGSPANS AS WIDE AS THREE FRISBEES.**

Children in **ANCIENT ROME** played a game similar to **LEAPFROG.**

COLLEGE STUDENTS
CREATED A PIANO
OUT OF

bananas.

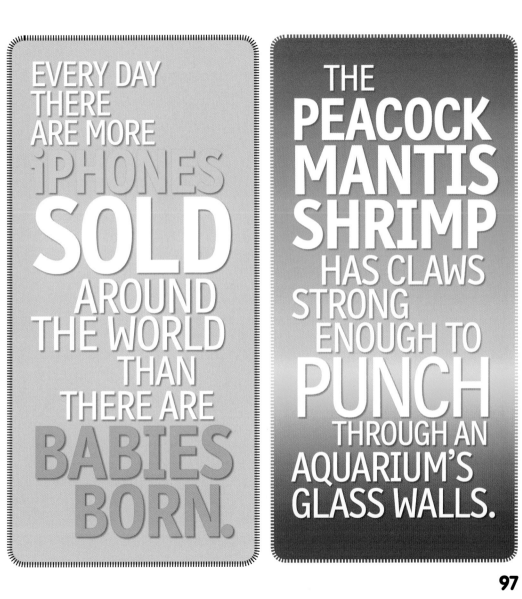

EVERY DAY THERE ARE MORE iPHONES SOLD AROUND THE WORLD THAN THERE ARE BABIES BORN.

THE PEACOCK MANTIS SHRIMP HAS CLAWS STRONG ENOUGH TO PUNCH THROUGH AN AQUARIUM'S GLASS WALLS.

MORE THAN **100** YEARS AGO, PEOPLE ROLLER-SKATED

BY STRAPPING **SMALL TIRES** TO THEIR FEET.

THERE ARE MORE **TORTOISES** THAN PEOPLE ON **SEYCHELLES,** A GROUP OF ISLANDS IN THE INDIAN OCEAN.

The word **suns** looks the same upside down and right side up.

It's possible to use a **smart-phone** to turn off the lights.

Soup made from **birds' nests** is a Chinese delicacy.

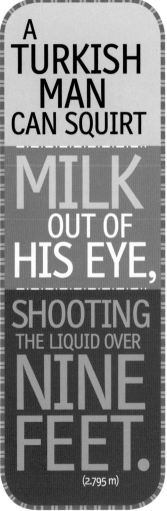

A **TURKISH MAN** CAN SQUIRT **MILK** OUT OF **HIS EYE,** SHOOTING THE LIQUID OVER **NINE FEET.**

(2.795 m)

LEGEND SAYS THAT PIRATE TREASURE MAY BE BURIED NEAR THE STATUE OF LIBERTY.

YOU CAN ORDER FRIED BONE MARROW FOR DINNER AT SOME FANCY RESTAURANTS.

THE U.S. POSTAL SERVICE MAILS MORE THAN 800,000 LIVE CHICKENS IN THE WEEKS LEADING UP TO EASTER.

Chili pepper crops grow hotter when there is less rain.

104

IT'S POSSIBLE FOR **A CROCODILE** TO EAT A SHARK.

SOME SPIDERS' BRAINS EXTEND INTO THEIR LEGS.

BEAGLE + BOXER

BOGLE

THE INSIDE OF A **CUCUMBER** CAN BE UP TO **20 DEGREES F COOLER** (11.1˚C) THAN THE OUTSIDE AIR.

·Your **lips** don't **sweat.**

CRACKERS ARE NAMED FOR THE CRACKLING SOUND THEY MAKE WHILE BAKING.

THE MWANZA
flat-headed agama
lizard resembles
SPIDER-MAN.

One type of Australian orchid spends its entire life underground.

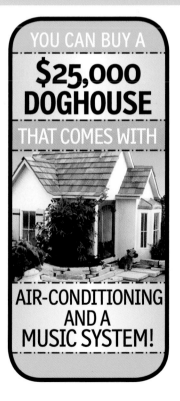

YOU CAN BUY A

$25,000 DOGHOUSE

THAT COMES WITH

AIR-CONDITIONING AND A MUSIC SYSTEM!

NIGHTTIME RAINBOWS ARE COMMON AT YOSEMITE NATIONAL PARK IN CALIFORNIA, U.S.A.

MOST
TORNADOES
OCCUR BETWEEN
3 p.m. AND
9 p.m.

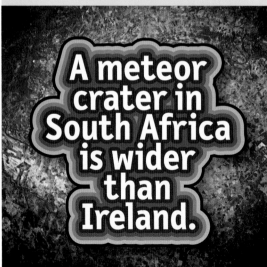

A meteor crater in South Africa is wider than Ireland.

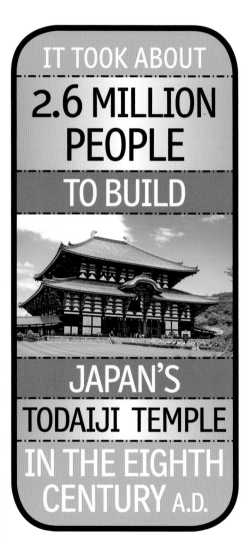

IT TOOK ABOUT

2.6 MILLION PEOPLE

TO BUILD

JAPAN'S

TODAIJI TEMPLE

IN THE EIGHTH CENTURY A.D.

A platypus **swims** with its ears and nostrils shut.

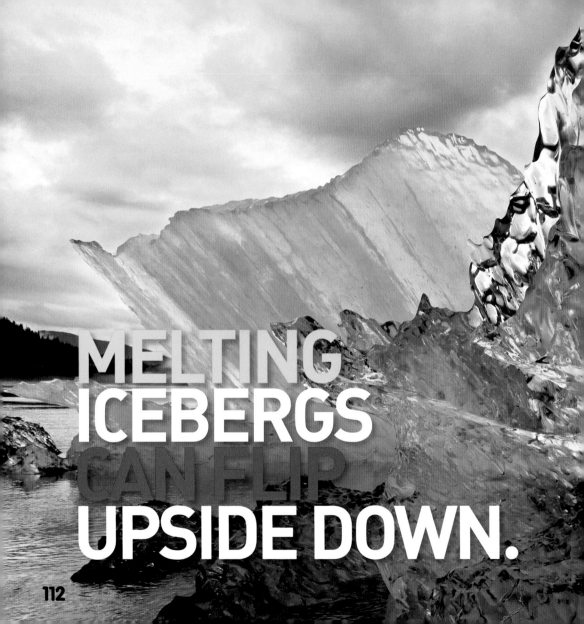

MELTING ICEBERGS CAN FLIP UPSIDE DOWN.

Fireflies can glow yellow, green, or orange.

A BOARD GAME WAS FOUND IN KING TUT'S TOMB.

TUBEWORMS CAN LIVE FOR ABOUT **600 YEARS IN THE DEEP OCEAN.**

THE AUSTRALIAN LYREBIRD CAN MIMIC CAR ALARMS.

One million pieces of sporting equipment were used during the 2012 Olympic Games.

An asteroid named **Vesta** is home to a **mountain** more than twice the size of Mount Everest.

BILLIONS OF YEARS AGO, EARTH REACHED **3,700° F.** (2,038°C) THAT'S SEVEN TIMES HOTTER THAN A BARBECUE GRILL AT A COOKOUT.

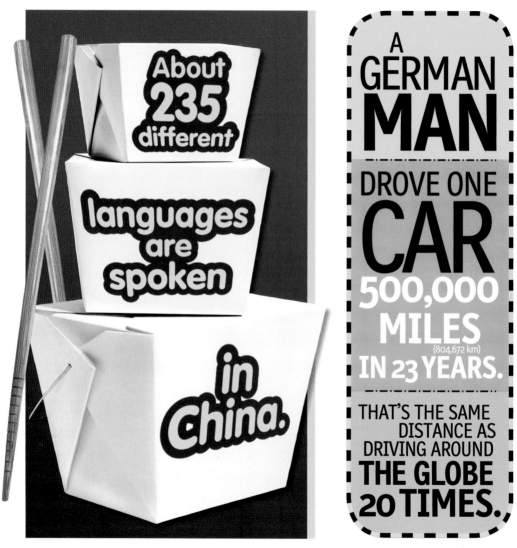

About **235** different languages are spoken in China.

A GERMAN **MAN** DROVE ONE **CAR** 500,000 MILES (804,672 km) IN 23 YEARS.

THAT'S THE SAME DISTANCE AS DRIVING AROUND **THE GLOBE 20 TIMES.**

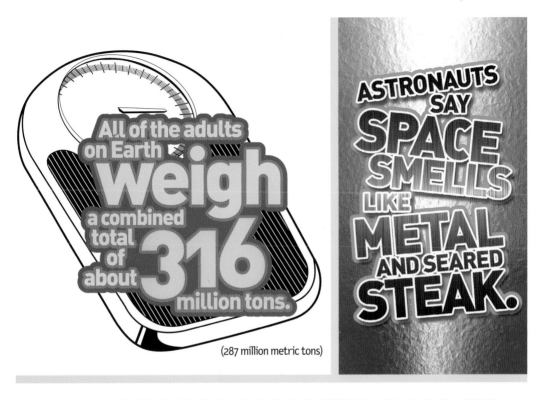

All of the adults on Earth **weigh** a combined total of about **316** million tons.

(287 million metric tons)

ASTRONAUTS SAY **SPACE SMELLS** LIKE **METAL** AND SEARED **STEAK.**

PREHISTORIC SNAKES, CALLED TITANOBOAS, GREW AS LONG AS SCHOOL BUSES.

RHINO HORNS ARE MADE OF THE SAME SUBSTANCE AS HUMAN FINGERNAILS.

IT'S CONSIDERED → RUDE ← TO WRITE IN RED INK IN PORTUGAL.

The Antarctic icefish has clear blood.

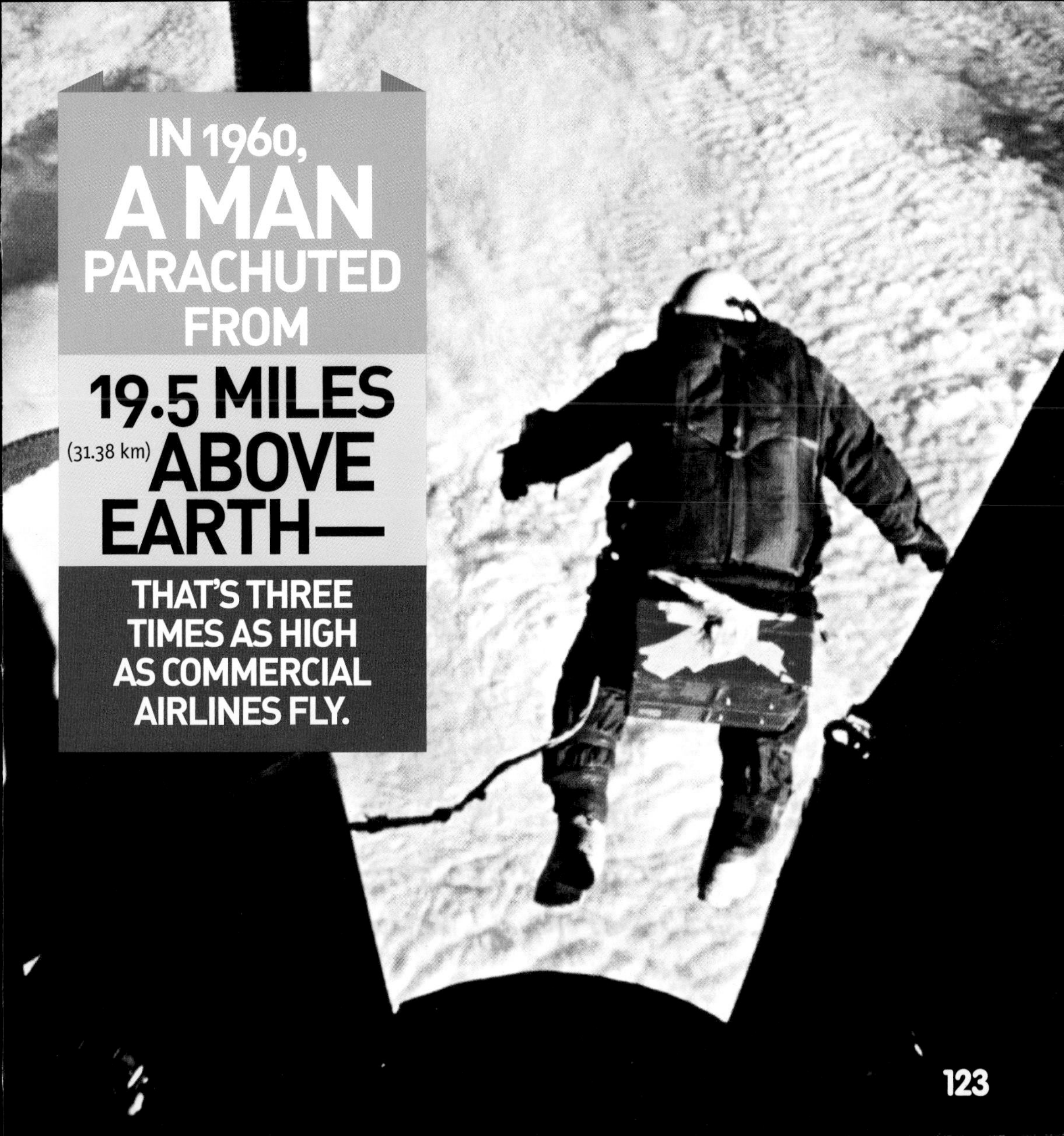

IN 1960,
A MAN
PARACHUTED
FROM
19.5 MILES
(31.38 km) **ABOVE
EARTH—**

**THAT'S THREE
TIMES AS HIGH
AS COMMERCIAL
AIRLINES FLY.**

A LEMUR
CAN WEIGH AS LITTLE AS
FIVE QUARTERS
OR AS MUCH AS A
CAR TIRE,
DEPENDING ON THE SPECIES.

CANADA PRODUCED ENOUGH **MAPLE SYRUP** IN ONE YEAR TO FILL **13** OLYMPIC-SIZE **POOLS.**

SOME WALLABIES HAVE LIGHT PURPLE FUR.

A SALTWATER CROCODILE MAY KEEP ITS MOUTH OPEN TO HELP ITS **BRAIN STAY COOL.**

There is a **sneaker** with built-in **screens** that **display** Twitter messages.

IT TAKES **65** TONS (59 metric tons) OF PAINT TO COVER THE EIFFEL TOWER.

IN THAILAND, PEOPLE HAVE **WATER FIGHTS** TO CELEBRATE NEW YEAR'S.

THE FLAP OF
SKIN UNDER A
**MOOSE'S
THROAT**
IS CALLED
A BELL.

There was **no ice** in Antarctica 55 million years ago.

IN SINGAPORE, PEOPLE WERE ONCE *FINED* FOR NOT FLUSHING PUBLIC TOILETS.

THE **RHINOCEROS BEETLE** CAN LIFT **850 TIMES** ITS BODY WEIGHT.

Ancient **Maya warriors** hurled containers full of **hornets** at enemies.

THE BODY WEIGHT OF A **SUNFISH** INCREASES

60 MILLION **TIMES** IN ITS LIFETIME.

(AT THAT RATE, A HUMAN WOULD GROW TO WEIGH AS MUCH AS FOUR *TITANIC* CRUISE SHIPS!)

A **KOMODO DRAGON** CAN SWALLOW A GOAT WHOLE.

There's a **90** percent chance your **parents** will **steal** some of your **Halloween candy.**

SCIENTISTS HAVE RETRIEVED **800,000-YEAR-OLD ICE** FROM A **GLACIER** IN ANTARCTICA.

A POPULAR SOFT DRINK IN THE UNITED KINGDOM IS MADE WITH DANDELIONS.

134

SOME **BAOBAB TREES** IN AFRICA ARE MORE THAN **2,000** YEARS OLD.

ATLANTIC HERRING

SOMETIMES FORM SCHOOLS THE SIZE OF NEW YORK CITY.

YOU CAN FIND MORE THAN **1,000 ANCIENT DINOSAUR** AND REPTILE FOOTPRINTS ALONG THE "DINOSAUR FREEWAY"— STRETCHING FROM COLORADO TO NEW MEXICO, U.S.A.

A half-inch-long (1.3 cm) **flatworm** has **60 eyes.**

THERE'S A **RADISH** THAT LOOKS LIKE A **WATERMELON** ON THE INSIDE.

A GUENON MONKEY'S WARNING CALL SOUNDS LIKE A **LOUD SNEEZE.**

THE **HUMAN BODY** CONTAINS A TINY AMOUNT OF **GOLD.**

A home run in baseball is also called a **"tater."**

DETROIT RED WINGS HOCKEY FANS SOMETIMES THROW **DEAD OCTOPUSES** ONTO THE ICE RINK **TO CELEBRATE A WIN.**

THE **EARTH** ONCE SPUN 0.1 MILLISECONDS FASTER EACH DAY FOR TWO WEEKS.

A REINDEER'S **NOSE** HEATS UP **AIR** ON THE WAY TO THE **LUNGS.**

ROASTED ANTS ARE A POPULAR **SNACK** IN COLOMBIA.

AN 18-HOLE **GOLF COURSE** LIES BETWEEN **TWO RUNWAYS** AT AN AIRPORT IN ASIA.

PEOPLE CREATE HUMAN TOWERS UP TO THREE STORIES TALL AT FESTIVALS IN SPAIN.

When you're driving on the highway, the **car engine** is *hot* enough to **cook** *a piece of* **chicken.**

There's an annual beauty pageant for camels in the United Arab Emirates, a country in Asia.

A **sloth** can take one week to **digest food.**

144

The number **4** is considered unlucky in China.

A 25,000-YEAR-OLD FOOTPRINT WAS FOUND IN A FRENCH CAVE.

Strawberries are members of the rose family.

A TYPICAL AMERICAN **GROCERY STORE** IS STOCKED WITH ABOUT **50,000 ITEMS.**

A REDWOOD TREE CAN PRODUCE UP TO 100,000 SEEDS IN A YEAR.

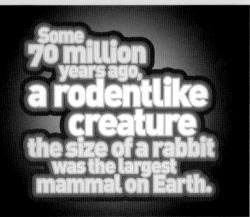

Yawns are more contagious among family members than among strangers.

Some 70 million years ago, a rodentlike creature the size of a rabbit was the largest mammal on Earth.

Elephant seals can stay underwater for up to **two hours.**

IT'S TRADITION FOR **NASA ENGINEERS** TO EAT PEANUTS FOR GOOD LUCK DURING SPACE MISSIONS.

THE AVERAGE **HOME** PRODUCES MORE AIR POLLUTION THAN A **CAR.**

There are about **14 million** fake **Facebook** accounts.

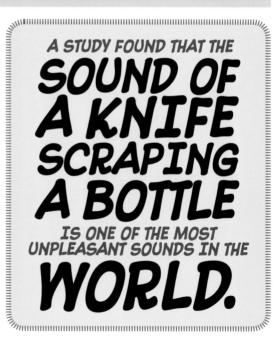

A STUDY FOUND THAT THE **SOUND OF A KNIFE SCRAPING A BOTTLE** IS ONE OF THE MOST UNPLEASANT SOUNDS IN THE **WORLD.**

AN **ALBATROSS** CAN **GLIDE** THOUSANDS OF **MILES** WITHOUT **FLAPPING ITS WINGS.**
(kilometers)

YOU CAN WATCH A MOVIE IN A GRAVEYARD AT THE CINESPIA THEATER IN CALIFORNIA, U.S.A.

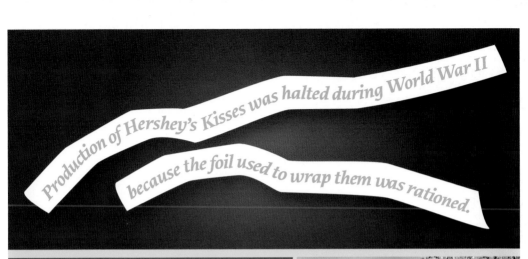

Production of Hershey's Kisses was halted during World War II because the foil used to wrap them was rationed.

In Bulgaria and Greece, nodding your head **up** and **down** "means **no**."

A WOODPECKER PECKS A TREE AT 15 MILES (24 kph) AN HOUR.

DOGS HAVE THREE TIMES MORE

TASTE
BUDS
THAN CATS.

YOUR **BRAIN** REMEMBERS 10,000 SCENTS.

IT'S POSSIBLE FOR YOU TO **SPOT THE LIGHT OF A CANDLE** FROM 14 MILES AWAY.

CHILDREN'S **HEARING** IS MORE **SENSITIVE** THAN ADULTS'.

YOUR STOMACH CAN EXPAND TO 40 TIMES ITS SIZE.

THE SKIN ON YOUR HANDS IS THICKER THAN 15 SHEETS OF PAPER.

YOU HAVE ABOUT 17,000 TOUCH RECEPTORS IN EACH OF YOUR HANDS.

YOUR BODY CAN DETECT TASTE IN JUST .0015 SECONDS— THAT'S AS FAST AS A BLINK OF AN EYE.

BUBBLEGUM CORAL IS BRIGHT PINK AND CAN GROW TALLER THAN A TWO-STORY BUILDING.

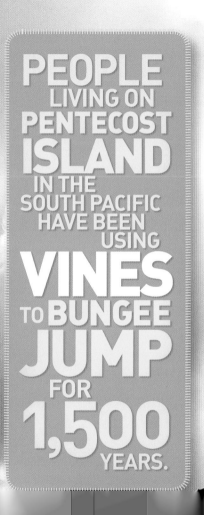

PEOPLE LIVING ON **PENTECOST ISLAND** IN THE SOUTH PACIFIC HAVE BEEN USING **VINES** TO **BUNGEE JUMP** FOR **1,500** YEARS.

BLUE-RINGED
OCTOPUSES
CAN POISON
HUMANS.

Alpaca moms **hum** to comfort their babies.

Swiflet birds' nests are made entirely from saliva.

THE AVERAGE AMERICAN GENERATES MORE THAN FOUR POUNDS OF GARBAGE (1.8 kg) EACH DAY.

Canned tuna is one of the most popular pizza toppings in Germany.

SOME ANTS CAN WALK UPSIDE DOWN.

Gelada **monkey calls sound** like a person saying **"yep, yep, yep."**

THERE'S A PLACE IN VENEZUELA, SOUTH AMERICA, WHERE **LIGHTNING** FLASHES UP TO **280 TIMES** AN HOUR.

FLAMINGOS DON'T TURN PINK UNTIL THEY ARE ABOUT TWO YEARS OLD.

The **Mississippi River** sometimes flows **backward** during powerful hurricanes.

The **iPod's name** was inspired by this line from the classic movie *2001: A Space Odyssey:* **"Open the pod bay doors."**

SNAKES DO NOT HAVE EYELIDS.

Nepal is the only country in the world that doesn't have a rectangular flag.

THERE'S A BEACH IN HAWAII WITH GREEN SAND.

SOME TAPEWORMS CAN GROW TO BE 40 FEET LONG (12 m) INSIDE HUMAN INTESTINES.

Some 75,000 pounds of meat sank (34,019 kg) on the R.M.S. Titanic.

Yak hair was used to make **wigs for** characters in **The Hobbit** movie.

HALF OF THE **PIGS** IN THE WORLD LIVE IN **CHINA.**

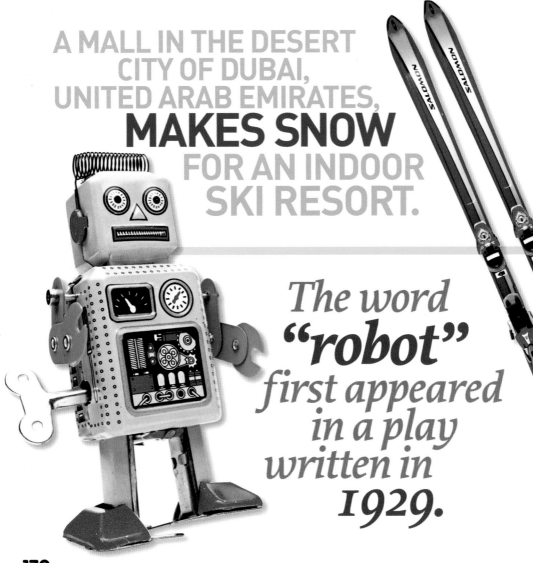

A MALL IN THE DESERT CITY OF DUBAI, UNITED ARAB EMIRATES, **MAKES SNOW** FOR AN INDOOR SKI RESORT.

The word *"robot"* first appeared in a play written in 1929.

THE AVERAGE ADULT TELLS ABOUT 11 LIES IN A WEEK.

There's a forest of crooked trees in Poland.

A CANDY COMPANY MADE A CHOCOLATE LOLLIPOP THAT WEIGHED 7,003 POUNDS— (3,176.5 kg) AS MUCH AS A HIPPO!

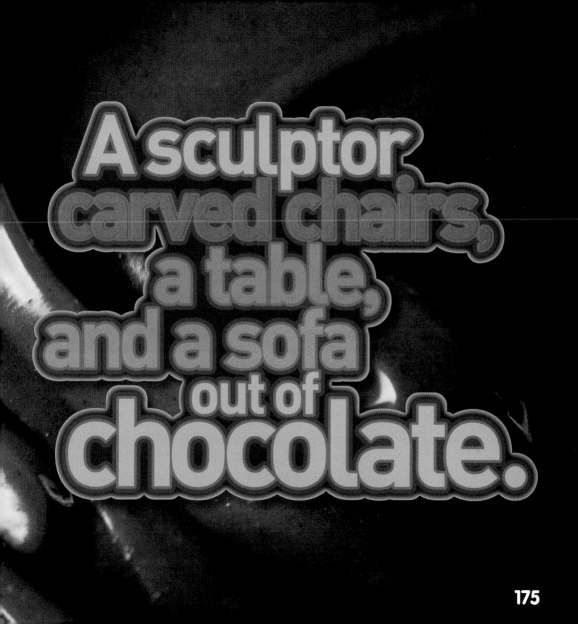

A sculptor carved chairs, a table, and a sofa out of chocolate.

New York City Marathon runners consume a total of **4,500 pounds** (2,041 kg) of elbow macaroni at the annual marathon eve dinner.

THE 1938 COMIC BOOK IN WHICH SUPERMAN FIRST APPEARED SOLD FOR $2.16 MILLION IN 2011.

SPACE JUNK—

MAN-MADE DEBRIS FROM SPACE—

FALLS TO EARTH NEARLY EVERY WEEK.

Two people separated by **600 miles** (966 km) *can see the same* **shooting star.**

TRAINED OPERA SINGERS CAN REACH NOTES ALMOST AS LOUD AS A JACKHAMMER.

The most popular password on the Internet is "password."

THE **PINOCCHIO FROG** IS NAMED FOR ITS **NOSE** THAT CAN INFLATE AND GET **POINTIER.**

ELEPHANTS
CAN HEAR
EACH OTHER
TRUMPET UP TO
FIVE MILES (8 km)
AWAY.

THERE'S AN ARTIST WHO CREATES TINY PORTRAITS ON
HIS FINGERS.

THE "EVERGLADES PIZZA," SOLD IN A FLORIDA, U.S.A., TOWN, IS TOPPED WITH FROG LEGS, ALLIGATORS, AND PYTHON FILLET!

ONE IN THREE PEOPLE SNEEZE AFTER LOOKING AT THE SUN.

SOME SAUROPOD DINOSAURS' NECKS WERE SIX TIMES LONGER THAN A GIRAFFE'S.

183

HOT-AIR **BALLOONING** WAS ONCE AN **OLYMPIC SPORT.**

A Chinese student designed a *postcard* that can capture the *smell* of your *favorite food*.

THE POPULAR TEXT MESSAGE ABBREVIATION, **OMG** FOR "OH MY GOD," APPEARED NEARLY **100** YEARS AGO IN A LETTER FROM A BRITISH ADMIRAL.

Early jack-o'-lanterns were carved from **turnips, potatoes,** and **beets.**

There are seven quintillion, five hundred quadrillion grains of sand on Earth.

ROBOT JOCKEYS RACE CAMELS IN SAUDI ARABIA.

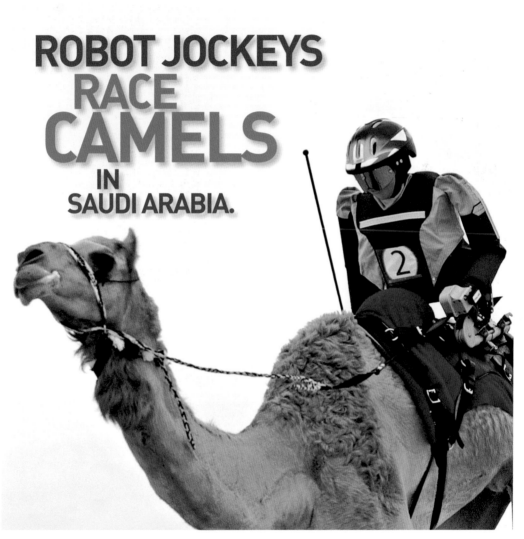

2 micron

6,000 TIMES LARGER THAN IN REAL LIFE!

THE WORLD'S TINIEST GUITAR IS SMALLER THAN A SPECK OF DUST.

IF ALL OF THE **DNA** IN YOUR **BODY** WAS LINED UP, IT COULD **STRETCH** FROM **PLUTO** TO THE **SUN** AND **BACK**.

Google was originally called BackRub.

A man made a **bike** almost entirely out of **cardboard.**

A CAT NAMED **TUXEDO STAN**
RAN FOR MAYOR
OF HALIFAX, NOVA SCOTIA, IN CANADA.

BEES ONCE MADE **BLUE AND GREEN HONEY** AFTER PICKING UP COLORFUL **WASTE** FROM AN **M&M'S** FACTORY.

191

THERE'S ENOUGH ENERGY IN **ONE GALLON** (3.8 L) OF GAS TO CHARGE AN iPHONE FOR 20 YEARS.

A pumpkin has been chucked more than a mile by a cannon—a world "punkin' chunkin'" record! (1.6 km)

The planet **Uranus** was almost named **George.**

A **restaurant** filled an aboveground **swimming pool** with more than **13,780 pounds** of **pasta.** (6,251 kg)

There are more **vending machines** **in Japan** than there are people in New Zealand.

ONLY 0.1 PERCENT OF BACTERIA ACTUALLY MAKE YOU SICK.

Less than **2 percent** *of the world's population has natural* **red hair.**

WHALE WASTE IS AN INGREDIENT IN SOME EXPENSIVE PERFUMES.

You're **more** sensitive to SMELLS when you're hungry.

CAPTAIN CRUNCH'S FULL NAME IS HORATIO MAGELLAN CRUNCH.

The sky above the **moon** is always black.

Lady Gaga has a group of **ferns** named after her.

A MAN SNOWBOARDED ABOUT 17,500 FEET (5,334 m) DOWN MOUNT EVEREST.

Squirrels **sweat** through their **feet.**

Yuma, Arizona, is the sunniest place in the United States.

Grass looks greener to girls than it does to boys.

The U.S. President's plane, **Air Force One,** has never landed more than **3 seconds off** its scheduled arrival time.

FACTFINDER

Illustrations are indicated by **boldface**.

FACTFINDER

T

T. rex **4–5**, 5

Tabasco sauce 39, **39**

Tapeworms 168

Tarantulas 49, **49**

Taste buds 57, 154–155, 157

"Tater" (home run) 140

Taxes 66

Teeth 30, 52–53, **52–53**, 67

Television remotes 7, **7**

Text messages 186

Thermal vents 43, **43**

Thunder, fear of 76–77

Titanic, R.M.S. 168

Titanoboas 121

Todaiji Temple, Japan 110, **110**

Toilets 7, 32, **32**, 129

Tongue 78, **78**

Toothbrushes 67

Tornadoes **46–47**, 47, 110

Tortoises **100–101**, 101

Touch receptors 157

Trees, crooked 172, **172–173**

Triceratops 30, **30**

Tubeworms 115, **115**

Tuna 163

Turkey (bowling feat) 80

Turkeys (bird) 20

Turnips 186, **186**

Turtles 43, **43**, **100–101**, 101

Tut, King (Egypt) 115

Tuxedo Stan (cat) 189, **189**

Twitter 73, 127

2001 (movie) 166, **166–167**

Typewriter (word) 13

U

Uranus (planet) 192

V

Vampire bats 37

Vending machines 12, **12**, 193

Venus (planet) 56

Vesta (asteroid) 117, **117**

Vision 156, 197

Volcanoes 56

W

Wagons 81, **81**

Wallabies 126

Walt Disney World Resort, Florida, U.S.A. **58–59**, 59

Wars 19, 129, 153

Water 13, 80

Water fights 127

Waterfalls 31

Weddings 37, **37**, 66

Weight 37, 121, 124, 131

Whales 24, 60, **60**, 80, 193

White orcas 48, **48**

Wigs 50, **50**, 169

Wildflowers 31, **31**

Windshield wipers 14

Winter, full moon 40

Woodpeckers 153, **153**

World War II 153

Y

Yaks **168–169**, 169

Yawning 147

Yosemite National Park, California, U.S.A. 109, **109**

Yuma, Arizona, U.S.A. 196

CELEBRATING
‹125›
YEARS

The National Geographic Society is one of the world's largest nonprofit scientific and educational organizations. Founded in 1888 to "increase and diffuse geographic knowledge," the Society's mission is to inspire people to care about the planet. It reaches more than 400 million people worldwide each month through its official journal, *National Geographic*, and other magazines; National Geographic Channel; television documentaries; music; radio; films; books; DVDs; maps; exhibitions; live events; school publishing programs; interactive media; and merchandise. National Geographic has funded more than 10,000 scientific research, conservation, and exploration projects and supports an education program promoting geographic literacy.

For more information, please call
1-800-NGS LINE (647-5463) or
write to the following address:
National Geographic Society
1145 17th Street N.W.
Washington, D.C. 20036-4688 U.S.A.

Visit us online at nationalgeographic.com/books

For librarians and teachers: ngchildrensbooks.org

More for kids from National Geographic:
kids.nationalgeographic.com

For information about special discounts for bulk purchases, please contact National Geographic Books Special Sales: ngspecsales@ngs.org

For rights or permissions inquiries, please contact National Geographic Books Subsidiary Rights: ngbookrights@ngs.org

Published by the National Geographic Society
John M. Fahey, *Chairman of the Board and Chief Executive Officer*
Timothy T. Kelly, *President*
Declan Moore, *Executive Vice President; President, Publishing and Travel*
Melina Gerosa Bellows, *Executive Vice President; Chief Creative Officer, Books, Kids, and Family*

Prepared by the Book Division
Hector Sierra, *Senior Vice President and General Manager*
Nancy Laties Feresten, *Senior Vice President, Kids Publishing and Media*
Jonathan Halling, *Design Director, Books and Children's Publishing*
Jay Sumner, *Director of Photography, Children's Publishing*
Jennifer Emmett, *Vice President, Editorial Director, Children's Books*
R. Gary Colbert, *Production Director*
Jennifer A. Thornton, *Director of Managing Editorial*

Staff for This Book
Robin Terry, *Project Manager*
Sarah Wassner Flynn, *Project Editor*
Eva Absher, *Art Director*
Rachael Hamm Plett, *Designer*
Callie Broaddus, *Design Production Assistant*
Julie Beer, Michelle Harris, *Researchers*
Ariane Szu-Tu, *Editorial Assistant*
Hillary Moloney, *Illustrations Editor*
Grace Hill, Michael O'Connor, *Associate Managing Editors*
Joan Gossett, *Production Editor*
Lewis R. Bassford, *Production Manager*
Susan Borke, *Legal and Business Affairs*

Based on the "Weird But True" department in *National Geographic Kids* magazine

Manufacturing and Quality Management
Phillip L. Schlosser, *Senior Vice President*
Chris Brown, *Vice President, NG Book Manufacturing*
George Bounelis, *Vice President, Production Services*
Rachel Faulise, *Manager*
Nicole Elliott, *Manager*
Robert Barr, *Manager*

Want more?

These books are PACKED with extraordinary FUN-tastic facts for the SUPER SENSATIONAL YOU!

AVAILABLE WHEREVER BOOKS ARE SOLD

Find us at Facebook.com/NatGeoBooks